WALKING AMONG THEM

WALKING AMONG THEM

Max Winter

Subpress
Ohio California Massachusetts
2012

Copyright © 2012 by Max Winter
Published by the Subpress Collective
ISBN 1-930068-54-9
Cover design by Max Winter

Library of Congress Control Number: 2013934526

Grateful acknowledgment is made to the editors of the publications in which these poems first appeared: *American Letters and Commentary, Boulevard, Colorado Review, Columbia, Cutbank, Denver Quarterly, Explosive, Failbetter, First Intensity, Iowa Journal of Cultural Studies, Jacket, Jubilat, Kiosk, Lit, Mississippi Review, Parthenon West, Pleiades, Ploughshares, Seneca Review, Sentence, Slope, Spinning Jenny, Tarpaulin Sky, The Boston Review, The Hat, The Iowa Review, The New Republic, The Paris Review, The Prose Poem: An International Journal, Typo, Unpleasant Event Schedule, Volt, Washington Square, Western Humanities Review*. Also, I am grateful to the editors of *Free Radicals: American Poets Before Their First Books* (Subpress, 2004) for including "As If I Knew," and to the editor of *New Young American Poets* (Southern Illinois University Press, 2000) for including "Long Distance."

The Subpress Collective was founded on the contributions of 19 people who donated 1% of their income for three years.

CONTENTS

ONE

Pendulum	13
Along With Me	15
A Door Falls Open in the Desert	19
Far Be It	21
Landing Time	23
What I Would Give Myself To Be	25
Suppose	26
Draft Of A Map	27
Walking Among Them	29
Eulogy	30
As If I Knew	31
A Secret	33
Hope, Spring	34
The Burn	36
We Did Not Decide, We Did Not Allow	37
They Say From This Valley You Are Leaving	38

TWO

My Blue Heaven	43
The Rose At The Hem Of The Door	45
Come In, Please	47
Suite	50
Now	53
That Is The Way	55
Apocrypha	57

THREE

A Follow Up Years Later	61
Breaking The Swear	65
Letting Go	67
On The Rails	69
If I Were You	71
How It Was Then	74
Of Course I Will Work The Lobster Shift	75
A Fit	76
Post	77
On The Way	78
Unforgettable	80

Space Parable	82
In The Altogether	84

FOUR

The Myth Of Polonius	87
Drawing It Up	89
Creche	90
That Night	91
Cosmology	93
Where We Have Been Found	94
Beware, He Bites	96
The Future	97
Pouring	98
Spring	100
Airborne	102
Saccade	104
O	106
Mice	107
Underdream	110
Not Seeing	111
It Cannot Be Believed	114

For Lisa

ONE

PENDULUM

As I was going to St. Ives,
I met a man who ended his sentences
as questions whose answers were all
"9"
because nine is three times three
and there were three of us:
me, the asker, and

As I was going to St. Ives,
I met a man who jingled change
in his pockets, as he talked.
But he had no shoes, and his shirt was ripped,
and dirty, and

As I was going to St. Ives,
I met a man who carried paper clips
in a paper bag, for clippings
snatched from gutters or trash cans.
But there was no one to make the trash;
I had thought we were
the last people on Earth:
me, the gatherer, and

As I was going to St. Ives,
I met a man carrying a bundle of sticks.
I asked him where he was going:
"Around and around," he said.

"From there to here.
And when I return, I will go around again,
until

As I was going to St. Ives,
I met a man who had six wives.
And each of those wives had six children.
And each child had six rattles.
On Tuesday they shook their rattles together
and deafened the church, and deafened the crows
that clung to the corners, and deafened the traveler, and
I

ALONG WITH ME

- I rode out through the desert
- Over and out it
- As I rode through the desert
- It was riding through me
- The place I was going was only one
- The man I was after was only one
- Only one man sitting in a shadow
- Sat in a shadow beside a black mirror
- A black mirror and a broken house and nobody near
- The man I was after was nobody near
- As I rode through the desert
- As it rode through me
- I followed instructions
- The notes from the start
- The start of the track
- That led to the man that was one
- One of those men in an empty house
- One of those men you might look for
- Look for like me
- Riding through desert
- Riding through me
- The instructions said to follow the purple
- But there was no *purple*
- And there was no *follow*
- There was only a *the*
- The house
- The track

- The man
- The desert
- But I rode through the desert
- I trusted the *the*s
- And the dust traveled through me
- Its grays and its blacks
- And its blues and its oranges
- Could lead to a house
- Could lead to a man
- Could lead to a mirror
- A purple
- A lonely
- A man that was one of those men you might look for
- Out in the desert
- Out with no map
- Out without safety
- Just lonely
- No mirror
- No grays and no blacks
- No blues and no oranges
- Just me and the track and the man and the night
- And I kept myself silent
- No speaking
- Just howling
- Coming from purple
- Not coming from me
- Where was the purple

- The purple seemed closer
- Closer than farther
- Further from me
- Than the man that was one of those men you might look for
- If angry or lonely or following orders
- Or thirsty from days in the Panhandle sun
- Followed by days in the old western sun
- Followed by days in the cloud fighting sun
- Followed by hours in a cave with the thought
- The thought of his nearness
- The fright of his nearness
- The smell of a gunshot
- Without sound of same
- Hours in a cave with the thought of a gunshot
- The thought of the same
- The thought of the desert
- The desert riding through me
- Riding through purple
- Riding through howling
- The howling of the blues and the greens and the yellows
- No speaking
- Just howling
- And me and the man
- In the house you might look for
- In the covered black mirror
- In the dust

- In the purple
- In the desert
- In fact
- It was riding
- Through me

A DOOR FALLS OPEN IN THE DESERT

I dine on the quiet light of the stars.

If I were to stop here,
my life would roll down the asphalt
by itself.

A cactus bent double.
A bone gnawed by mosquitoes.

The red on the swinging door,
ripped by occasional white.

I am neither at the center
nor at the end.

I speak less
than the sand does
when the wind blows.

A headless snake.
A paralyzed river.

I keep my Bible
in a box,
my truths
in a trunk.

A mesa takes the shape
of a hat
tipped.

FAR BE IT

They took away my moving sidewalk.
They would not tell me why.
I guessed that when questions arose
on relativity in daily life
and I remained silent
although I knew the answer, my problems
commenced. I flew low that day
over a field in Denison, Texas
where two odalisques were drinking Orange Julii.
Some outsider begged me to give them a wink,
to be not happy with what I was.
I sighed and stepped up
atop the streetlight later that year,
exerting a pull upon the moon
like the strength of 39 million extras
in a film about the tiny and the mammoth
and who would win if a fair fight were held.
Whatever the cause,
the smiley faces rained into my stillness
and the burly man of Idaho
came to me and offered me a place
beneath his emblazoned umbrella.
He was wild with friendliness;
I felt I had met a high pressure system
or some light precipitation, or both.
I peered into the storm of wrong heads
at the glimmer I knew to be the last train

to the final ferry to the brink.
O Cheyenne! You have the face of an incurable thirst
in overalls, nice breasts, no shirt. Lead me not.
I handed up my ticket, drank faintly nutty coffee,
and tried to find plateaus
in the leavened evening,
moving ever towards what once was half the world.

LANDING TIME

It was raining when he landed in the unflappable city. The sun had almost set. The air inside his taxi was dark gray, dark blue. He wondered how he would traverse the city without a car as rain fell on green shrubs, green lawns, green porches, green cars, and green streets covered with pink blossoms. Funny that the rain had not flooded out the city by now. Nothing was cleaner for the efforts of the falling water. Everything, on the contrary, was dirtier, as though debris were falling from a dust pan somewhere above his head. His mission was clear enough, although he did not know how to begin completing it. All his efforts at sketching an outline on the airplane had been interrupted by flashing white clouds beside his window. He also kept nodding off and dreaming half-dreams of his project, laid out for him by an unintelligible but dulcet voice. He never saw the face behind the voice, assuming it belonged to someone at the other end of his trajectory. He woke from these naps with aches in his head. In fact, his temples smarted in the taxi. The radio predicted that lateral precipitation would graze the metroplex, that barometric pressure would hover, and that residents could expect to see temperatures drop. His cellular phone rang. He pressed a button marked "Listen" and put the mechanism to his ear. And all he heard was susurration, possibly waves, against what beach he could not tell. The sound continued for thirty seconds and then the line went dead. He pressed and re-pressed "Listen" several times but did not hear the sound again. No matter, his hotel was a few hundred yards ahead, facing the ocean. He left the cab and found his room with no trouble. The bedspreads, the carpet, the furniture, and the wallpaper were all an immaculate white. He turned on his television, hung from the ceiling by four thick chains. On two channels in a row, wolves ran across tundra; on a third, masked men cursed softly as they explored an open chest with knives and tubes. He pulled back the papery curtains at his ceiling-high window. The boardwalks by the sea were completely empty. Recalling that he needed to contact the Committee, he walked to the rightmost bed and picked up the phone. The line was utterly silent. Upon going downstairs, he found no one working behind the reception desk, although the guest book was full of names. Down a hallway leading off the main lobby was a door bearing the words "The Sea of Tranquillity" in Gothic lettering. The door was unlocked, the room itself dark. Once switched on, the cobweb-covered chandelier revealed only a large empty room with a bar set up against the far wall. The cab driver had said nothing of a national holiday, or even a bubonic plague. But had there been a cab driver? He didn't remember paying. And hadn't he felt like a bear in a shooting gallery as he walked through the empty corridors of the city's municipal airport? And hadn't he felt a curious sense of relief when he discovered the large number of empty seats on the airplane? The doors of the hotel were wide open, by now; gusts of rain had soaked the nearby carpet in a dark red semi-circle. He walked straight ahead, towards the fathomable and undulating sea.

WHAT I WOULD GIVE MYSELF TO BE

Roosevelt tells me loudly and clearly what I am doing wrong. A rat crawls across the stage. Out in the open city. The terms are absent or unnecessary. Someone is not telling me the truth. Terrible thing to lose your mind. Orchestral backup for the dropping of lead. What lead. How foolish could I have been. On the curtain is written the name of a typhoon. In quavery letters. She likes me, she doesn't, she likes me, she doesn't. Big Roosevelt head on a small Roosevelt body. Is this important. Do I wake. George Jones descends from the wings. Am I George Jones. George Jones is not singing but shooting. Pick a peck. A cough. Sleigh bells. It is a long way, over the tundra, dirty and indistinct dogs, where do they live the ones I love. Long hut. Ranch house. Shadows on blinds, on shades, too much snow to pick someone out. Is it snow or sleet. What's funny. I say again. All my flies are zipped. In the house the cider. A crowd a-smother. Pipes a-knock. Two koala bears nuzzling my cuff. A kick and a kick and I cannot kick them off. I run through a thinning white. I sense that it is not mine. Which is why I cannot escape. Rumor. Levity.

SUPPOSE

A man's life is not his own. The silverfish have taken it to earth. He spends his days in the luminous corridor. "It's round," he says. "It smells like blood." His life may be leaning against the wall. He knows so little. Early one morning, he passes women sitting beside a lake. A woman with midnight lips comes close: "What can I do to help?" She leads him. The room is familiar. The man tending bar is an angle or two. "Give me a glass of water before I drown." The music changes from a waltz to a mazurka. A chance to cut losses. But then his guide asks for a dance. It's a dance you might have seen in a film: spinning this way, he feels almost drunk. When she lets go, he flies back, but not into chairs or boxes. It seems too long, this time he spends falling. When he wakes he is clawing his way out of brambles. The air wears the smell of a portent. Even the earthworms seem to know. He sees smoke on the horizon. He walks towards it, wanting to think there is a city, there is a village. When he arrives, he finds men warming their hands. He examines the burning effects. They are his. The shadow boxes, the model castle, the costume dramas. He watches his shadow rise on what might be wheat, white in what might be darkness.

DRAFT OF A MAP

The way in which things don't always make too much sense. Could, if you would turn your head away from the clearing. Songs in a rattling sort of progression. Useless for the new method. The idea of the unbidden rest. In the middle of the bridge. The idea of daylight. Someone's laugh in a glass cage. Buried beneath the sand. Coming up the stairs. Screw it on to the top, now next. The shoe chops into the pool. Life and the myth of Tantalus. Hair on the Bible, and the room not checked out of. A tear. A screech. The letting go of the ink, along with the sound. A flit discernible in the cool shadow of the bridge. No preparation. Every possible dream, and this the grommet. Where are we the archetype. The patchwork invisible. A thank you to you and also to you. Made of lettuce. The ache. A singe for a breath. Two no's added to a yes. The relent made into a tee-shirt. Push them out. Make them stand up in this Antarctica. I was fine for a while, then I became Sunday, almost fleshy. The sleep came to the little town a ways from home nestled in the choo choo valley a bye baby. The need to manipulate or at least touch. This a building? That will climb up to the sky? I am lying in the dark. Pleasure on your lips. A window half open. A practicum in my lap. It was precise only once. Then. Soap on the brain. A sample of each person's perspiration. Taken back to the back. Enveloped in a folder. Sealed with a kiss. They were all against us in the pandemonium. They were tearing us to common sense. It was a sad stretch of the country, dotted as it was by silver mines and dead men. I am a passenger, and I ride and I ride. It was calculated in the well beneath a hand on a cool gray table. Dudes on the sidewalk next to muses on the lawn, and where were we in the illustration? If I wanted to find the ferry landing. Empires in error. A ghost of a mushroom a blessing in the absence of a pen to write something down. Keep tucking, and don't forget under the bed, too. Fantasy after function. Hunt the elk in the light after. Trumpets watching over your scalp. The signal, not this pause. This rest after the crackles. What was it for, the passion? Assumption, presumption. A brown smelly sack, is where. Two little pigs. My love is pulled up. The clock is set.

WALKING AMONG THEM

I cannot tell you the whole story because the whole story will not fit in my mouth. I have always had a small mouth, small tongue, tiny lungs. If I were to try to tell the whole story, I might expire. All over you, and you in your best black robes. It's like trying to swim with one arm towards a waterfall, not moving very quickly but swept along anyway by dint of being in the river in the first place, instead of back at the farm, where the lights are just high enough, and the sounds just soft enough, that you can hear yourself think. But that's all you ever hear. But why would I have moved? Why would I have gone out towards the glade, why would I have kept on when the ground began to sough, why could I not pick up a branch and hold it? Was the wind such a graceful comer? Could the thickets have pushed me with their clamor and their tinted sunrise? Could the water have made such an offer? What was I thinking? Or was I chanting? I was neither, with my bucket and my pole. I was merely carrying a small light into a future month. Leaving spectral crumbs. So that what I did would be clear to everyone. Or it might be something not yet done. I might keep my arms outstretched, eyes squinted, a circumspect semaphore. The troops would know by themselves where to gather, the generals where to put their x's.

EULOGY

I could ignore things once. She loves her pursuer like a comet loves a lens. She looks at me as if I were a milepost. She wants to know what I do not know myself. If I could move, I would explain. But the last time I moved was when I was made. I let my maker choose this prudish position. Because I would die within hours, how I lived them could not matter much. The lobster eaters cannot grasp that a shift in the seat is the mark of a king. I wish for anything that looks like life. I would like to run and dim the great chandelier. The right gesture at the right juncture could interrupt or end the celebration. The diners could wander home through the hand-shattered sky. Slip into my blind spot, slip into the foyer, but do not laugh. Place a hand at my hairline, a hand at my jaw. Take what remains of me, put me in a bucket. We can still escape to what is not. Yet. I will melt, and I will flow downhill, but the wind and the air can take care of that. Take me to the back of the world. Drop me. At this rate, I will never know the difference.

AS IF I KNEW

It was a good year, he says at the top of the new hotel, in the room always lit, in the room in which a television always plays "The Dahlia," in which a flower is the voice of a death, what voice it can muster in the crackly noplace;

it was a good year, he says, lying on his bed, hands outstretched, in one hand the model of a small city—where we may find an apothecary ever to grind in a pestle, an architect to build Valhalla, an optometrist to let us Through—and in the other the wrapper from a box of cigars given to a box of friends;

it was a good year, if you take out the bad, he says, as the snow picks up, as predicted from blue fields on the edges of weather; and the guest can see less, but he looks less as one meeting begets another meeting, as more water is drunk, as a series of figures keeps him from his train;

in which the living room is empty till the murderer enters, the sound is running behind, mouths move, the ending will not satisfy;

if you take out the bad, you are left with the following figures, he says;

where we pray beneath the bells, where we play some old records when the houses are empty;

if you take out the bad, having loosened his tie, having dropped his shoes, having picked up the phone;

it was a good year, he says from the top of the new hotel, to his absent, to the Wood of Suicides, to the Bellhop;

in which a flower is a piece of candy, in which a face is a piece of contrast; the film may stop as an object may stop, mid-sentence;

if you take out the bad parts, sure it was fine, maybe with changes; the glass he has held will fall on the ground;

in which brambles grow at the scene of the crime, in which everyone knows, all the time;

goodness gracious, the killer done struck again

A SECRET

I have a breath
I keep in my pocket
for when I hear boots
walking over my head,
making cracks in the ice.
The word for this sensation
is tangled in anemones
and unnoticed by divers.
Only one person in the world
knows its exact location.
If the word is ever unearthed,
rewards will fall like snow,
no two alike,
none lasting longer
than the time it takes them to catch
on the threads of a glove raised by accident
to wave to a dark figure
moving across winter,
a wave from one thought to another.

HOPE, SPRING

I have not slept
and yet I am happy.
I have spent the whole night
listening to straight lines clattering on my desk,
covering each other up.
They cannot help falling,
it is as if they have been pushed
from behind the gauze curtains
and although they vanish almost instantly,
there's a story in the descent
like flower petals soaked in water
to make a sort of invisible ink
readable only by foot-bound princesses.
What I have been trying to do
is be one of those princesses,
although my voice is too deep
and my footsteps too heavy on the snow.
It keeps you awake or at least in hopes,
a matter that turns itself over and over again
without ever connecting parts to your liking.
Thus entangled you walk out to the country
in hopes that an answer will pick you up
and the radio will be well awake
and you will rattle singing into the yellow-pink continuance.
But if it doesn't happen, you fall in love,
as I have, with the first thing you see,
which is in this case a dead chimera.

Its head rises like a foreshadow
in the perpetual musky dawn
even as I have taken a rod and lifted
this simple cranium up to greet us, even as I push
the thing back to the water. I'm wise enough by this hour
to know this is a beginning,
if not of a city then . . .

THE BURN

The glass metamorphoses
when the cars rise
on a Tuesday,
on Church Street,
beneath the phantom basket of gray drops,
and a breeze unbuckled.
I am tasting an idea,
raw and uneasy, almost squirming,
and drinking water doesn't smooth the hitch
in my programme,
nor does accelerating the porch fan.
The yard goes wild
as I lose my age
in a paperless act you would have missed.
The telephone man
has his back turned,
45 feet above the yard.
He listens for something else. He is not my species.
My eyes close, as
what was
recedes.

WE DID NOT DECIDE, WE DID NOT ALLOW

Great men poled the boats downstream. The elephants pulling the barges moved quickly towards the coasts. Then the stir. Every face went down for one minute. Nothing happened but everything changed.

I boiled water between two walls all the while. I talked like fire to those who listened. My employers could have told me the time was ending. Not enough to send me home to sleep. I could have helped things along.

As bananas fell from the sky, we were all considered happier. A latch came unstuck at the bottom of an hour. Old friends joined once again. As I re-established myself, a breeze blew beneath my feet. The loch of days began to fill with barters.

Four dimes for a song in the old blue box. Seven dimes for a ginger beer. Four dimes to keep our grandpa quiet. Seven dimes, seven lilies. Four dimes at the bottom of a dropped pocket.

THEY SAY FROM THIS VALLEY YOU ARE LEAVING

Going to hell in a hand basket
doesn't take much time;
you start on the reedy shore
west of where it all began,
at the end of the access road
lined with lawn chairs and older men
walking unsteadily into shallow ponds.
You'll push off without goodbyes.
You'll sit up straight. You'll keep your eyes open,
mouth shut. Branches will burn
on either side of you, lighting
the warp and woof of your basket,
constructed slowly by ungloved fingers.
Your first moonrise will be the most blinding.
You think you'll never see again.
But soon you will see all the time,
even when you're sleeping,
even when you stare at pitch blackness
demarcated only by falling frogs
and the basket-handle stretching above you,
a dark space in the blazing night.
Now and then moss will glow,
and you'll wish the holder of this flashlight
would appear and push you back.
But your basket will slide into the shadows,
following the path drawn in shaky marks-a-lot
that leads to the end of the line—

and you'll know the moss was two centuries old,
not worth the chase, and the only tasks left for you
are silence, floating, and understanding . . .
When you arrive and begin to stretch
your legs in the blackened weeds,
you will taste this house
on the back of your tongue.
When you have let yourself into the starlit foyer
and found your way to the back kitchen,
there is just enough room
for your head to bow, slightly,
and you will hear a low song
from behind the empty cabinets.
You will hope that someone is coming.
With light or water or a pinch or
a slap in the face to wake you.
But no one is coming.
In the end there is no one here but you.

TWO

MY BLUE HEAVEN

I should help myself. My spirits are still asleep. My eggs have been cooked. Not in sunlight but in steam. When you remember me, be sure to note my high, intelligent forehead. My thoughts run from east to west. From cheek to cheek. I have begun to think visibility would be a good idea. This from someone whose contentment is exceeded only by the size and dark shade of his blinders. Let me have another piece of toast. Let me have a napkin. My habits at this hour run to sloppiness. Four out of five psychologists, scratching themselves through ratty underwear, testy at being awakened for a merely human question, report that sleep deprivation leads to unhappiness. But is it not true, doctors, that unhappiness and weariness are one and identical: weariness of trains, weariness of hardwood, weariness of October, weariness of gusts, weariness of baked apples, weariness of one's own sexual organs, weariness of Avenue A, weariness of bed, weariness of talking to some ever-distant person? But I am not an unhappy man. I simply slept little and woke early. The reason was not you or I or it or them or we or me or his or theirs. Alice kept me awake, floating above me, a chiding ray in my autumnal forest. I chanted, "We live to love and love to live and love to live and live to love," but I could not achieve the stasis I needed. I needed. But that's bubbly in the topsoil. Let it fizz. Let me have another cup of coffee, now that you've peed. Your full thighs and urban smirk are almost enviable. Almost. I do not depart my heliport so easily these days. You see, I have other concerns. I am covered with hopping and un-killable green bugs. Or I must be. Not to complain. No one likes a complainer. But I've begun talking to the stars. They don't move around so much. They're optimists. And they've performed steadily for many years. Venus is my favorite. Venus, like night, is always available. And all of you who know me, all of you who think you know me, I'm never coming around here, never again, no more. Brando? And there goes the tram to Roosevelt Isle. When I was invisible, I thought spotting the tram meant good luck. But at this point it means the ambassadors are going home. The ambassadors have left. The ambassadors are no more. Alice brought me here and told me she didn't know me. That I felt nothing for her. I told her she wasn't watching, I felt things for her at every crosswalk, for every thinkable and unthinkable reason. And then her tongue in my ear. Where is that tongue? But more importantly, where is that ear? I must find that ear. I guess I should settle it up. Less of a tip than a transom through which my generosity thoks on the counter like a letter that says, "This will have to be the end of it all," and if you wake up crying in a cold water bath, who ever finds out? Ninety cents ought to do it. Okay, a dollar. And I leave you, Greeks, picking eggs from my molar. And I walk out. Oh, it's still dark. I turn to the right, and a little white light, will guide me to my, blue, heaven.

THE ROSE
AT THE HEM OF THE DOOR

Sometimes he would imagine her blond and barely covered crotch, other times her freckled breasts, sometimes just a wrist or forearm. They hadn't spoken much. He constructed several conversations, each one ending with a kiss that tasted like burning newspapers, burning letters, three fires in three fireplaces. And maybe some coffee. She once wondered aloud if he had read everything, because he seemed so diligent and alien to her; he said he didn't, and then he spilled coffee on his jeans. His brother said the rose meant he wanted in her pants. What in her pants? Her knees? Her shins? One of her thighs? Both of them? He didn't place the rose in her pants. No, at her door, Room 502. It was 7 A.M. when he left it. He didn't hear anything, so he assumed she was sleeping, maybe on the bare stomach of a close friend, as he had heard. And soon she would sleep beneath the petals of a rose. When she saw it in the hall, she left it there, went back to bed, tried to sleep it away. A rose with a note with his name at its foot. The note explained nothing but his name; she wasn't even sure the rose was hers. The air was so cold as he walked to the market after; he stared at fresh fruit for an hour; he was afraid he had changed everything. They saw each other after dark, at a small and open gathering; she thanked him, and said it made her feel better, although it didn't, really. Larger, maybe, or more watched. Better than what? He tried to imagine what distant lake might have drowned her, what morning she watched in his face. Always watched, every time she passed him and his oddly square shoulders in the street, always looking straight ahead. He did inspire her, in some way, an unrealized option, an unvisited home. And he did have relatively rosy cheeks. But all he watched were her lips. And occasionally her eyes, placeless; he'd heard she'd grown up all over, seen all kinds of things. But who knows what she saw, and who knows what she said, and who knows what he said? Their chats could not be timed or recorded. No one knew a thing. And the rose certainly didn't know, crushed and broken as it was; she'd stepped on it by accident, and then stared down at it, wondering how she would explain the sudden injury, and then realizing she wouldn't need to, because he might never speak to her. All his studies gone to a wink. And even when drunk he could not speak for long. One day, he would run into her in a clearing, in the park, where all the leaves had been swept away, a place everyone normally ignored. The river would lie to the east, the city to the west. She would have slight shadows under her eyes, speak less than she normally did, maybe a bit overworked. And he, too, would be abnormally silent, wondering where all the leaves had gotten to, and wondering if she had kept, if she had thought to keep it, if only for the sake of feeling better. And then it would occur to him that, in the final analysis, the wind would probably blow the rose away, that none of this would matter in the end, not matter at all. And she would look, strangely enough, up at the paring-away oaks, unable to find the right moment to speak, unable to make anything work better, or more efficiently, too bad she had fallen asleep, too bad she had stepped so carelessly. What to do, really? He was probably wondering what time it was.

COME IN, PLEASE

Your hand
turns the till of the ship
that tugs the string
that pulls the globe.
With my eyes closed
in this upstairs room
I have proven it
to myself.
We are acquainted,
but are we acquainted?
I have cut my own hair.
Let me show you these pictures
from the world I occupied,
always in front of a two-way mirror.
It would be nice to just snack
and if you would like to stay
you may.
Of course, I was alone once
and could be alone again
with no troubles but fruit flies,
they rise so far in this city.
As you can see,
I was a wild kid.
But here,
in a row,
are the prizes I won.
I cut my hair

and I could cut yours, too,
some Sunday.
When I drink milk
fast, like you,
I grow large,
and when I grow large
I walk
when I would prefer to float.
Do you see this mark?
I think of myself these days
as a guest
in a very fastidious world.
Oh take these cookies
and throw them out the window!
I'm sorry—are you cold?
Would you like some pie, heated up?
They heat my room
with steam, in pipes
that knock, at night
when I should be sleeping.
Who has the patience to boil all that water?

I hear you are an author.
I am an author, too, or was.
Does your apartment have exposed beams?
Are we acquainted yet?
Don't be bored—

more tea?
The wind blew these receipts
off my bedside table
and I didn't think
to pick them up.
Do you care about the papers
that cover the floor?
Or are you
casual?
Have we been
acquainted?
Is there a plain of ice
beneath your skin?
In the dark I can't tell.
I'm sorry.
Do we know each other,
now,
or do I talk
into a box?
My chair? Bolivian.
My hat? Armenian.
The staff? Kenyan.
My scarf? Icelandic.
Your cup? Welsh.
This shoe? Italian. Of course.
In the dark I can't see
where I put the rest.
Pity I have nothing left.

SUITE

I.
"Or do they sit in dark theaters?
Or do they find unrequited love?
Or do they drive into the glare,
minds moving on buildings that reflect?"

II.
The telephone drops from your hand.
If you let it dangle further,
its wire will unwind
but you will have no chance to speak.
As if you were not your current incarnation.
As if phantoms did not circle you,
scared themselves that something in the air
might be lost beneath the heartbeat—

III.
Your favorite color has lost its cap.
But you will not let me look for it.
In fact, you act as if you didn't notice.
In your painting of the world, Cuba has been erased.

IV.
You draw yourself lifeless,
you draw yourself naked,
but nowhere in your approximations
is a glimmer of the old brick underlay.

But to be fair, you let me under your umbrella
when the planets were falling like hailstones.
Do you remember that day?
My eardrums would not stop bursting.

Try the chiaroscuro of this cup.
Try a mushroom from this plate.

V.
I've never been so glad to crack a window!
I thought I might become a thought balloon
that could hold only one exclamation point
To float from this tendentious frame
into someone's bedroom, a space hidden by a newspaper

VI.
or already elided by an unexpected guest
O thank you for teaching me to waltz
The classroom is covered with sawdust
doctors have named it the human eye

I call it a presidential suite
It surely means nothing to you
but I must learn to dance before the carnivals begin
I am convinced when I am thinking and alone
that someone need only loosen the screws
holding the slats that block in the playroom

All I do is move back and forth
Boil water
Wait for the day to come

NOW

I write at the cuff of the world.

I catch myself drifting, and would think to be a man. Would the poem of woman differ from the poem of man?

That the poem of woman would be standing and the poem of man sitting, legs and arms crossed.

Must be one different from the other. One of them must be humming with ripeness,
the other just. Not. Cannot be both.

The women who watch me start to open their programs. They would speak at a high pitch if they would opt to speak. But they would not opt in this darkness. There is room only for my rhetoric.

Because I am the woman speaking and I am the woman writing the poems. Not to be too fine.

There is a man, after all. Out watching me like a mantis. The only thing putting him from me is I loved him once.

Some would say they go away. Staring at the seat before him. Wonders where I am, why I do not sit in that traveled seat. That is not my question. I did not begin that in him.

But he asks now, look at the mess. Piled so high. It hides her eye. Have you seen that look before?

I feel nothing as I listen but a tapping on my ear. As if a stray dog nuzzled at it. Freshly escaped. Freshly filthy.

It began as a tiny thread, he says, and grew into a whole catastrophic skein.

(Do not listen. He is only one of many.)

We were laughing when we lay the great gray cubes, he says. The great gray cubes are hard as flesh. I know them, he says.

(I reckon you. I thank you. No one goes home without a bruise. What would the world be, anyway.)

Or maybe that's not it.

THAT IS THE WAY

I had thought I could say these words
but you had run across the street
and I could not go where you had gone

This is where it often ends
A moves towards B
only to find that B
was only pretending to be in a place
where A might reach it
No,
B has realized the shortcomings of the first place,
and though A may not realize them,
B has no intention of sharing
the secrets of the second place

This will affect the last count
if the light is bright enough
If not, it will make us anxious
(and I am sorry, there is no remedy,
maybe taking a drink of water, looking up
into the dark live oaks, but guarantees are not mine to give)

Because we are always A,
always in the middle of being left,
or if we should happen to be B,
it is only for a moment,
and a curtain falls over everything soon after,

gives no pleasure in the taking of that moment,
is almost surprised that pleasure was expected

APOCRYPHA

Long ago
two cloud-covered hands
uprooted the street,
from its ball park to its lawns,
and cracked it in two,
leaning the halves against each other
to form a bridge.
I loitered under the arch
to read the notes left there
until a train passed through,
pressing me against a mossy wall.
I could hear laughter, telephones ringing,
the rustle of wet hair shaken dry,
that was all. When I left the tunnel,
wiping chalk from my clothes,
I found the bridge, the hills, and the lake beyond
covered by one long shadow.
When I looked upwards,
I was surprised to discover
that you had arrived already,
that you wanted someone to take your bags,
that you had waited seven years,
that you might not come again.

THREE

A FOLLOW UP YEARS LATER

The day
sits
on my tongue
and slurs happen
as they do
sometimes.

But what bothers me
is what is happening
down there
where they live
and some of them work.

The size of the hole does not decrease.

It seems I expected otherwise.

Some things
some people
cannot be found
down there.

The people who are looking
will stop looking
from sheer old-fashioned numbers
and the people who are not looking now
will find themselves there

at a time they cannot determine.

Here
where gardens grow by themselves
no one knows.

Or maybe they do.

You would imagine.

I would not speak.

One man I know
went west
one woman
went south
another
gambling
another
did not move.

I cleaned
listened to Don Giovanni
whose spirit has never been
more a push
up a slide
more a nudge.

As well as I know his lines.

Even so.

The journalists asked
if I cried
if anything stopped.

No. I spat
shook
on my back
on the sofa
on the ground
sleepwalking
and all but no
I never cried.

The journalists say
it is the start
of the finish but no
I am trafficking
in another medium
stakes planted
in another country
another backdrop.

That winter I listened

to French music some
and read simple French sentences.

That was all I accomplished.

Thank you France
for not going anywhere.
Thanks also to
Switzerland, Sweden, and Monaco.

If I can't take myself away
or cannot be taken
I will bring this about.

Until the wheel
is once again
minded.

Do you understand?
Do you forgive?

BREAKING THE SWEAR

The one
who blows himself apart
makes secular gravity
in which
one body is not
heavier than another
but all bodies are
in due collision
with other objects,
seen and unseen.
When special ink
falleth from heaven, the moment
is visible. As has been seen
in dens and living rooms,
you need special instruments
to make it like anything at all.
Only a few selected children
saw the last touching.
Ah, but they could not understand.
Of them all, only
Katya Rodriguez O'Houlihan
read the signs,
could talk the tongue of glow and crash.
And when she spoke,
she talked not about the parts
but about the whole, gone.
No one understood a word,

thinking she might patter instead
about a sport or an event
from the vivid red fire truck of film.
They thought she might have drunk
from the wrong idea,
in the wrong century.
And what did she know anyway,
of the man in the open brick world,
the breeze of without,
the little orange picture in his chest?
Did she not conceive
of the storm of difficulty?
Perhaps it was her past,
or perhaps she fell prey
to a roving conceptual scrim.
The light went on
and the glass kept flying
out beyond the westerly assumptions,
out beyond the cool outdoor accomplishments,
stopping by woods, at last,
chuffing into the gray
of the forest of sight.

LETTING GO

I would like a
stamp, a 90 cent European
air mail stamp.
I need to mail a
bomb today.
It's a small bomb,
not a
perfect one, but
its intent is sure.
I constructed it
myself, yes,
and I stuffed it
full of candy,
and I
am hoping
that you
will be able
to accommodate me.
I feel as if I know you.
I feel
as if
I know
all of you.
You anger me, but
I love all
of you just the same.
Where are you from?

I ask because I hear
trees in your accent.
Are you from a place
with trees
or without trees?
It makes a difference,
how things look
when you leave
a place.
Maybe you left long ago.
I did,
and I came
here.
I liked it
at first
and then I decided
it wasn't necessary,
any of it.
I know what I need.
Do you know what you need?
Is this it?
Is this?

ON THE RAILS

It was on the faster train
on Tuesday, in the middle of the morning,
when I should have been working,
that two men began to talk to each other,
really talk to each other,
both turned three-quarters outwards
to me, propped across the aisle,
behind a magazine.
One began to speak,
and then the other spoke in turn,
and it came out
that the older one
had been on the news, earlier that day.
I looked at him carefully,
and I remembered I had seen him, now, today,
that, in fact, he was part of the reason
I was on the train now, rather than earlier,
part of the reason
I was so very late.
The man who was not on the news began
to espouse his view on the vote
and the scattering and the burst,
and the man who had been on the news
listened, smiling and nodding,
every now and then expressing an insight.
The man not-of-the-news would rub the back of one hand
with the palm of the other, nervously.

My eye was drawn to the motion,
and I began to stare.
One rub, and then another,
as if one hand
were trying to make the other disappear,
as if the man who did not know the news
might want to vanish
at any moment.
And I continued to watch.
And I could see that the news man
was watching as well,
taken by this,
resting his mind.
And then he began to rub his own hands,
either in sympathy or of an independent spirit
diving for itself
in the middle of the morning,
where I, mouth opened just a little,
had arrived at my stop.
The train pulled, and then paused.
I rose
above them
in the space
of the car.

IF I WERE YOU

If I were you
I would be traveling
through space
the dark of olives
If I were you
I would not be
what I have been
for years
still
not I
but invariably
not you
rather something like them
the men in long fur coats
they who look like them
and not any other body
but a body of citizens
assembled in space
the dark of olives
traveling through space
the color of them
and not the color of I
that which I
invariably
have not determined yet
at times
the color of you

you as you appear
beside citizens
the color of olives
assembled in a they
that could not be called a we
because their voices
are not traveling through space
the color of I
not traveling through space
the color of citizens
assembled in a we
I speak
and that
qualifies as a movement
encased in a dusk
perjured by silence
a silence that I
and you
and we
and they
invariably
participate in
participating
through silence
through darkness
or near darkness
the color of long fur coats

the color
of a body
any body really
really not I
really not we
really invariably
traveling through
traveling
through
I
through
us

HOW IT WAS THEN

We were asleep in the weather.
The weather covered us
like an eye closing.
The eye was flurrying inside itself,
and were we asleep, or
were we only thinking
so hard that it felt like weather?
On our eyes and skin so long asleep,
so long closing with all the thinking
taking place, despite the life rising
above us, into the weather, through it,
beyond it, even, light through the eye
of a cloud until it became other than life
and we, asleep, could not have covered
it with a hand or a finger, said goodbye
to thinking and what thinking might become,
what weather it might bring upon the living,
what closing to those thinking or those asleep,
a quiet no to someone who wants to give rise
to something more than himself, beyond these thoughts
always closing like eyes, or even mouths.

OF COURSE I WILL WORK THE LOBSTER SHIFT

You, or not-you, spoke of a job. Did I hear things? Already, you leap about me like a small terrier. I am not a box of snacks.

The decomposition and rearrangement of astronomical bodies? That is my specialty. I can also bend like light, depending on the lens employed. During my days in fossil fuels, I thought I might be one. And then, when Luminone and Sons commissioned me, I became a telescope. I have been Everyone, more than once. All tasks one task, if you are me.

Of course I will work underground. Of course I will work the lobster shift. What, after all, do you take me for?

I will put my ear to work. I will hold my hand wide open, wait for the misplaced pellets to fall, and place them beneath my tongue.

A FIT

There has been an explosion in the allspice factory. There will be no more food today. Everyone goes home too happy to speak. The hats that fly to the firmament. Everything may be enjoyed. Absent lovers, you will never cry again. The coxswain in the forecastle has hiked up his garters and soon he will dance us a jig. For the city is gang agley, and we would be fools to sit happy. We cannot be tuckered yet.

When winter crawls around the earth, looking for its glasses, finding only twine and carpet remnants, a light will plow its way through hands that wave, a light will come and tell us. We will sit there in the half-dusty, half-blue air. We nod our heads and tap our feet. And from the hollow year will come a letter, a Christmas card left in the midst of fires. Open the card to find the undrawn face. It may bespeak, or it may snuff.

I knew there was no joy in restraint. I gathered the leaves with the names on their spines as the word struck high in the valley and the plain. I rose to pains beneath my back and caught my only glimpse of glory. You were there, all of you. You had made your accord, and you welcomed me. It was kind, but I was lost and gone. I played a musical saw as the leaves burned.

POST

One calls in sick. Another calls from the street. The last calls in, I can barely hear, says, "They are bombing my quarter today. I cannot possibly make it in to work." I look around me. What can I do? I cannot build the great ship without others to fit it together. I have a model, here, I've made out of toothpicks. I could show you what I expect. But the last time I showed you, you said there was thunder. But I hear no thunder now, just your voice. Saying "no you're crazy," falling off again until morning.

ON THE WAY

You were saying?

I need a tourniquet for my tongue. The press has broken me in two. I need a panacea. Someone must bring the lightness back.

Who can tell where the fracture lies?

I am too delicate to stand it. I am too angry to speak. I will never work again. They should have watched out for my writing arm.

If I touch you it's only for the sake.

Not there, there. Where the sun spots start. I have not seen much light. Like a certain blind frog I'm thinking of. Lived blank until the fuse was fixed.

I can read your mind. I have read the entries you have made.

You don't know me.

I deny myself nothing. The inside demands invention. Keeps it whole. If I could write my name. If I could write other things as well.

You know that I grow closer, and yet you persist.

Like the ocean knows a baby. Like a radar knows a storm.

Who will be the first to reach the bottom?

If this were that journey.

If I were the first.

If we could speak frankly, eye to eye.

UNFORGETTABLE

The thing he had in mind, the one thing,
leaves, chained to a wind.
He does not know where to look.
After a palatial hour,
framing figures that know no frames,
he walks to the window.
Many floors below him,
a park with wanderers inside it.
He could join them, it might give sense
where there was none before.
But then he realizes he does not know the words,
will be forever beside the sentry's box.
As shawls of cellophane fill the air,
he tries to return to the work,
telling himself that his mind
might have been working in secret.
A character, a young girl, has risen to the top of the tower.
In early autumn. In the oldest city on Earth.
On finishing that moment he started breathing,
he remembers, when she came to the top, all by herself,
and tried to find someone
in the black ink dots on selfishly small grounds,
and could not. It frightens him,
as the heat fails to go on,
that he might have dropped his chronic feeling of concern
in just another box, so quickly a part of the other
he makes each day, in gathering amounts.

And as it so happens, he allows himself once more to worry
that this work might be only a completion
of a work left unfinished in childhood,
not a calling in the silver screen sense
at all, at all; that the frames he makes,
the little sublimations, order as distraction,
the footprints, the comic clouds, the motion lines,
might form a small black-and-white city against him
in which he might find himself
dressed as a pig, flogged with wet rope,
cast out, even, the beneficiary of lost interest
that voices itself in chapels, in stage whispers, in excess,
What is this? What am I to it?
What have you done? What are you going to do?
It may strike him, at such a time, on such a day,
the opossum he called an idea having sunk into fakery,
that what he has done, will do, is wrong,
that he must stop it, check the bread.
And then he will hear a faint crack from outside
and get to the window in time for a tinkling cloud
rising where a frozen branch has fallen,
and he will go back to work,
and the somber smooth machine will tick again,
and the girl will fall to the ground in a box
but slowly enough,
blanks notwithstanding,
erasure an assumption,
uncertainty everything.

SPACE PARABLE

I had pelted the robot with all
manner of missiles but still
it would not give up the information.

Back in the pod,
I was held responsible
for the ultimate destruction of everything.

Even Professor Marienbad,
humbled as he was by invisible meteors,
would not receive me in his study.

I wiped the astral windshield,
scrubbed the neutron pots,
scoured the spoons with stardust.

My Airedale mug was broken while I slept.
My go-cart racing trophy lost its polish.
My letters never reached the planet Earth.

And then, for good behavior, I received
another walk on the fiery surface.
I thrilled at the chance—but went blank at the thought.

When I came to, I saw the robot
standing above me, shaking his head
with gravity, extending his map.

Like a punishment. Like my name was Rex,
or something. I grumbled to the easternmost crater.
I scribbled with a stick among the radioactive particles.

And they never heard from me again.
The ship went dim.
A world exploded its petals into space.

IN THE ALTOGETHER

That hair, fingers, feet fall onto my bedspread. Sing the right words, right now. The water that sweetsies through the grounds does not have the gift of sight; the coffee I drink drips from a sunspot; it cannot take away the night. But why would it? I ask the meter man that question, turns out I lose the lottery. I am late to work but work is light: light noise, light lifting. My bosses are drunk on Spanish champagne and the sky is the black of an armpit. I have heard the swords are coming on trains and porticos but now it more than seems the case. I have never cracked a heart in two. I have never stolen from a family business. I do not deserve these sharp looks. The mailroom clerk holds one hand out. Nothing comes in. When the thing occurs, every man is half the man he should be. The acts forbidden and forgone. The fires that wait and the fires that pounce. There are no forests left. I cannot call you; I cannot get away. No more walking backwards, into the sky. We learn not to trifle but to wade in the life that remains. Of that life, pick a secret third. Some of us keep working and some of us go down, all of a word. The city will crumble like a pastry. I'd say more if it weren't for the wings lingering. If it weren't for the fire after. A lot cast. What eats you.

FOUR

THE MYTH OF POLONIUS

Certain Peloponnesian statues
might converse for days without saying a word.
Nothing would pass between them
but occasional lost and snapping tourists
or blue herons headed for mystical paintings.
The unutterable is passing strange
with its union suit and clipboard,
standing in the doorway like an uninvited aspen,
but we must let it in
and we must buy its peculiar machine.
How else to get the bloodstain out?
When our guest has reached its daily quota,
I will come running with a glass of ice tea,
ready to trade up one stultified night
for an hour's worth
of whatever it has to say,
which ultimately will have to do with suds
at the bottom of an empty barrel,
turned on its side,
whose songless interiors reveal,
when the sun is two o'clock
of my right eyelash,
a reflection in oak of the muse's last photograph,
taken without her permission and published posthumously
in the interminable *Collected Letters*,
which I have sitting at home
but will not read because

I haven't the time to decipher its burning lines,
penned on the fly leaves of unnoticed minutes
and saved by the fellow in the Panama hat
who lingered by the piano
until the punch turned brown.
Life is short, and so am I;
let's leave this gathering
and stroll to the lake of darkness,
to the roadhouse and the jam session
held by insomniacs sitting in their underwear,
unaware that anyone else might hear them.

DRAWING IT UP

The Tallest Man In The World once told me, I get a charge from the threat. It starts in my stomach and ends when I end. Get it? I lost my Voice in 13 years, so I could not answer. I waved hello to the Diggers under our feet. The blue Glow above us was too much. It dropped heat on our heads, and in the middle of July, and in the Lower Antilles. A portent with no guts.

We stood on the stomach of the Fat Lady. She might roll us into Bedlam. She might take us to Bed. We laughed into our nutshells. We were the closest we would ever come to children. From my seat on the head of this sleeping Snake, I think of those days and stick out my tongue. We did not love Woman. Nor did we love Day. Nor Value. The Clairvoyant Piano could not point us to Town, even for a glass of German Tune. Truculent old clapshut was in the right. We should have asked the Wild Man Of Austria. One thump for Yes, two thumps for No, a small roasted boar for an everlasting Thus.

I woke at two last night to watch the Ifs flying across the Ceiling. I set my Clock three days in advance. I kept my Special Glasses holy clear. No one might get them but the Household Gods. Alas, when I came to the cold foot of Dawn, I found all bets off, all tents black and flapping. Like eyes reading a promissory sentence.

CRÈCHE

Fifteen or twenty plastic chalices
bounce down the fairway
of the tall aspen avenue.

A sibilant blizzard darkens a window.
A woman cuts her own hair
beside a lily of burning manuscripts.

No one tells the griffins when or where to perch.
No one tames the dogs with human heads.

A tongue slips at the back of a bar:
Is Christ here? At last?

And gospels keep rolling along
to the tune of the wind that freezes the grass.

From a broken aircraft I plunge
through snapping white light and into the arms
of Joseph, and Mary.

My flotation device is stuck.

THAT NIGHT

I saw something adrift.

It looked like a man to me.

It could have made my troubles disappear.

It made me ask questions I would not have asked.

It weaved through the clouds like a splinter.

Trailing nothing but the suggestions.

No words light enough to describe it.

I called you to the roof.

I showed you the shape of the new music.

You built a dome to catch the beats.

The man turned sideways to face us.

He seemed to wave, but it might have been the air.

I was not standing on Earth.
But I still believed in certain freedoms.

And my mind was no smaller.

Yet the world grew no smaller,
as much room as I gave it.

That evening, as I stood in the street,
watching a thing
trying for humanity,
flying short.

COSMOLOGY

The clouds do not move. But then I think they are moving. All along I've been misled. This is not stillness but a giant contraption. No one else looks. I could go. Out. Left. Towards the great and the burning. Are you among the burning? Is that where you went? You have to understand, nobody told me. No one has ever told me. I have learned what I know by reading your lips. In the dark, or at best by candle.

Nothing to teach me now but a dead thing on its back. I continue ascending, but where? I rise above the blond wood and the weave that curls and the dish that sings, "I'm pre-pared!" I don't know who to thank. The photo that might tell me shows too much. It could be edited. Someone could draw a circle. The image will last. Someone could direct viewers' gaze towards the center, where the answer sits smiling like an ape.

WHERE WE HAVE BEEN FOUND

Coming out of a small theater
in a blizzard
I am a box on legs

Is it a feeling or is it a mirage
We are often persuaded by size
to make certain internal connections

For me they happen with accumulations
of luster and reflection
I massage them until they are right

At least I cannot name a building
that has persuaded me, or even seemed to do so

When I experience buildings
I am going through, under or past them
and they make me want to stay at my post
But I cannot call it a persuasion
more an incentive
much like a taste you might want to reclaim
that haunted the side of your tongue
until it dispersed down a side street   gone into the wild

Where are you is the question of the day

They seem to ask it in the little well-lit shops

Of course I may not be listening
It seems like night but it may well be the end of grace
and I could be saying a number of things
but I have this sense that I am not

That inside a small wattled cottage
in the shadow of a mountain of junctures
dialogues and monologues are falling
from a small gray machine
onto the hard white floor
where they are not falling in any order

There was once an order inside the machine
but it was jettisoned to make room
for me, just me
All the way home my face is strangely red

BEWARE, HE BITES

They purply told him the boom had dropped.
They redly alerted him to a problem with the cash
flow. Someplace south of the wick a mound had popped,
under it tape of ticker, the last of the dark cache
from an ancient party. He did not go, but would flog
the trees with symbols of scrambled signalhood.
Poor nutwad, he was crowing like a log
when they came to him. They took him for dead
but then his opal lips began to move
and the wind upside the foothills came a rush.
Could the gnomes have invaded? Cabin walls stove
in like cheeks. His forehead ablush.
Everyone was summarily scared to death:
still no room inside the inn, even for a breath.

THE FUTURE

A needle points aslant the wuthering heights
behind the bookcase, west of the auburn door;
lookit. The snow is twittering. It lights
most of Rankin and some of Westminster. Anything more
and all the schools would close, account of an act of God
the blind can't address directly. They eat lunch
in the Varsity Diner (with some of the local fire squad):
an old Niçoise salad, Mrs. Inez's Blancmange,
and coffee. They talk quite loudly. You wouldn't guess
they'd have seconds, but they do, and they keep
tracing figures on the tablecloth, as if to question
an hypotenuse. Heloise loses her position. Heloise weeps.
No steam table. No Yahtzee. No silence for the deaf.
No one seems capable of finding the sheriff.

POURING

I think this condition will not last But I curse it Calling it a condition Only a conversation that will end without an eclipse to mark it

A bus passes this spot No crosses but in appearances

An approach comes over me Comes beneath me Others notice the change I no longer snap I no longer quicken

But when the approach is gone a foothold is no closer

We are locked into the house without walls The house moves without our say-so

I had it written down But a wind came along Undid my statement Made me comfortable in the head the waves make

I cannot limn the curvature of an immense accident

I cannot revise the terms of a punishment You make them up and they are permanent And then the gods return from the seaside Bodies pouring nowhere

My reservations are in check as of this moment You will never find them as we are falling

Out of California Up from the fish in the moldy alleyway Out of the no-city Out of the thought of spiraling air Out of twee melodies Out of the reach of a non-touch

And the reach that was supposed to happen By you By me By them The reach is replaced with a shrub Beautiful Final It speaks Or begins to But the rate has grown Does not allow for extended murmurings And this reminds me What did God say In what color Who did it belong to Who tugged at my religion Where had it been before it came to me To whom did I pass it like a sound

Such a thing could only be absorbed It could not be brought in a basket

And if I deny in the end we are falling If I deny that there is only one cloud above us Somewhere this side of the tower

We are falling and saying at the same time

Say the truth Say it here

SPRING

I am safe as a red brick house in my kitchen, no one here;
the air opens to tsuris and other cyclones,
great blustering cousins of the Apocalypse, rocking our huts,
or heats that make me smell sweat sweet,
or balmy nada afternoons of gingko, gingko, gingko
and staunch pagodas among the palms of the park
where I walk and sit after work subsides,
or maybe the hum of clouds that keep it to themselves,
or even light rain saying "It's okay it's okay" forever and ever.
Nothing's okay. If it were,
why sell road maps? Why mail the letter edged in black up north?
Because explosive clueless moths cluster at its edges?
The messiah never arrives, but not for lack of souls
to forgive with two, sweetly, fingers.
In Batman, the heads of state become mounds of dust.
In Beirut, you cannot say "ping" safely anymore.
I could give the world a small card: "It has always been thus."
But all I know are my seven feelings:
passion, jealousy, economy, curiosity, anger, boredom, passion.
Passion is the strangest thing. Where'd it go. Indeed.
I look like I'm crying but really,
my sense of whimsy has escalated,
and if, deep within a primordial forest,
I gargled with brook water touched by a sorcerer,
this pity and terror might end.
At home, before my Mirror, I am
a mystery play, a Devil, baptizing my tee-shirt

bathometrically with snot and water.
I try brewing some tea, but it fails to derange.
We're only alive for the length of a gulp,
and I spend it perched beside Formica,
drinking pale tea, drifting, never arriving.
The ultimate cup of tea may be coffee.
Else, it must be brewed with fresh water, the pot not watched,
I must use the loosest leaves, let no sound occlude
the whistle of the kettle, and not so much drink
as suck. The air enters with the water.
The air cools my burning tongue.

AIRBORNE

The wind exchanges itself
with itself
one afternoon
every afternoon
when I have been watching
the wind
and it has been watching
itself
trying to catch
itself
in a reclining pose
so winds can be
exchanged
brought out
handed around
in dirty hands
secretly
as if there were such thing
as if we were the wind
as if we knew the words
the afternoon catches
and tries to pawn off
a watch
a pair of dirty hands
winding it
a pose
the wind refuses itself

will not exchange
one for another
and yet continues to move
never catching on itself
never reclining
upright
for wind that is
upwards and back
every afternoon
at this time
on an incline
dirt flying
where I begin
to know
such secrets
as fly around
exchanging one place for another
explaining nothing
having brought nothing
to me
as can't be explained
in the time the wind takes
to exchange itself for itself
one afternoon
every afternoon

SACCADE

It is eighty degrees out here, says the clapboard

Heat becomes us

Grass and corn stop

A motor idles, knowing its battery is running out

A bookstore clerk makes the motions
and then decides not to make the call
A tryst framed in doubt
collapses into solitude

Wit struggles with witness
Witness wins, never smiling
Wit cannot sleep for a hundred years

An orphan becomes a parent
A child becomes a fixture
A fixture becomes a feature
A feature becomes an entire novel

Let us drag the corpses away from here

River? Ducks? Ghosts?
Who makes this request?

To search for a link between
earth and sky was pointless
                —even for the natives—
but they did it
and so I will too
                —find my phonograph—

Love is gone
Here is the cup it drank from
ringed and blotched in red
nobody's life

I am too old

to wake at noon
and yet the sun seems to be
trying to leave
through the back window
beside me, without me
as I doze

It may
I might
One could

O

I.
Sun raffled off. Long fingernails of cloud. Two topographical maps on the same dashboard. Route lost, battery dead, pomegranate crushed. Where is the other traveler? What faculties are left? Where is the loose mitochondrion? What makes you arrive home? (If no compliment is placed between two shoulder blades, on the ticklish part of the neck, in a niche that Memory scoops with her thumb in a wall of newly uncovered loam.)

II.
You take the rightmost of three highways, the one that leads to Memphis. (Anyone standing on a bridge can see it, squinting or no.) The sunshower is of consequence, falling in the alley, on the flat brown roof of the library, which collapsed once—no one thought to see it off into the open weedy lot of wrecks.

III.
Matisse aloft behind the couch. Matisse in the bathroom, taped simply on white. Impassive cedar, impenetrable patina. A bruise on the head from a branch thrown, no manners, by a boy who slipped momentarily out of his cloister within the City of God. Who forgot him if he did not forget himself?

MICE

There is a cricket
chirping in the county
next to ours
and would you please
go turn it off,
she mumbles at five
in the morning.
In the morning
he likes to sleep sometimes
but this morning
he lies awake
wondering
without bothering anyone
about the blender downstairs
in which he tried
to liquefy an onion
but only chopped it,
leaving a smell louder
than the cricket to which
she referred in soft tones
and then nothing from her.
Wondering then
about wondering
about it.
It is hot in the room
but there will be no air,
not yet,

not until
it stops leaking
green, yes green, foam
onto the shiny wood floor.
The ceiling fan ended
up in his dreams last night,
not working well though
it was, the squeak was
nine or ten animals
before he received his command.
You can measure the quiet
here, far enough
from the city,
by how loud
each new statement sounds.
It wasn't that he noticed,
and it wasn't that he answered,
and it wasn't for lack of love.
It was the world events
written about so nobly
everywhere, what about their crickets,
what about their blenders.
It was the galaxy deaths,
saying implosion to himself.
It was the shuffling
of pieces of earth,
the xylem and the phloem

processing water and food
with only sun for company,
the scheduled departures
later that morning.
Perhaps a light had been left on
somewhere.

UNDERDREAM

A crowd of shoulders waiting for a train
disperses, leaving only cups behind.
The reason why is unclear. Light rain
happens. The phone wire continues to unwind.
A man inside a sodden, latticed box
records this day with a screech
within, eyes angled towards the clocks
for life, and no one there to teach
him how to be a Taoist. But why bother? No trains arrive,
the shoulders are an illusion. All that's here
is a leafy lake surface, the scattering from a dive
a hand takes, the rain the splash we're
feeling on our cheeks on this July-ending day,
and the man in the box is only a box, headed Mexico way.

NOT SEEING

what it was
was
what it
was
and though it
was
was
what it was
was never what
was
was
somehow

where it is
is
where it is
so that
where is
is
not it
when I say it
I mean where it
is
with a nod to
where it
was

if
who
we
were
were
where
we were
when we
were we
we could not be
where
we were
if now
were then

if were were
who
and not where
if where were
we
and not
I

you would not be
am
I would be am
and also

is
sometimes

when where
is not were
or was
and is is not where
or a lone who
then I am

and then
I is

look up
the sky is missing

IT CANNOT BE BELIEVED

The fire hydrant painted white with black spots like a Dalmatian thinks, "I do not like your form of insincerity."

Arguing is useless, because who is always moving, cannot stop, even when sleeping?

Are either of you prepared to remedy the heat or the smell?

I thought not, from my biplane about to touch down on the mitigated potential of a city.

The reward for the completion of the mission is an untouched white petal.

It was born just above a folded hand.

The hand belonged to a famous poisoner, as fate would have it.

I have forgotten his name because, as at many times in my life, in so many ways, I did not record it.

It is a wonder to me that I maintain order.

It is a wonder to me that you are to be my wife, after all the freshly poured blacktop and all the Indian paintbrushes.

I did not think that I could give that place a picture.

It was the struggle of the scribes and the jongleurs, the joists and the boards, the hours and the doors that keep us out.

What will be the outcome of these new clouds breaking up above?

The emperor cannot do his own sums, nor should he.

That yesterday, I was a poorer man. It cannot be believed.

Max Winter's first book, *The Pictures*, was published by Tarpaulin Sky Press in 2007. He has published reviews in *The Boston Globe*, *The New York Times*, *The San Francisco Chronicle*, and elsewhere. He is one of the poetry editors of *Fence Magazine*, and he co-edits the press Solid Objects.

OTHER BOOKS AVAILABLE FROM SUBPRESS

Bentley, Scott. *The Occasional Tables.*
Bouchard, Daniel. *Diminutive Revolutions.*
Bouchard, Daniel. *Some Mountains Removed.*
Brennan, Sherry. *Of Poems and Their Antecedents.*
Carey, Steve. *Selected Poems.* (Ed. by Edmund Berrigan.)
Cariaga, Catalina. *Cultural Evidence.*
Carll, Steve, and Bill Marsh. *Tao Drops I Change.*
Davies, Alan. *Raw War.*
Davis, Jordan, and Sarah Manguso. (Ed.) *Free Radicals: American Poets Before Their First Books.*
Dinh, Linh. *All Around What Empties Out.*
Edwards, Kari. *A Day in the Life of P.*
Elliot, Joe. *Opposable Thumb.*
Evans, Brett. *After School Sessions.*
Fitterman, Robert, and Dirk Rowntree. *War, the Musical.*
Friedlander, Benjamin. *The Missing Occasion of Saying Yes.*
Guthrie, Camille. *Articulated Lair.*
Guthrie, Camille. *In Captivity.*
Guthrie, Camille. *The Master Thief.*
Harrison, Roberto. *Os.*
Hofer, Jen. *Slide Rule.*
Holloway, Rob. *Permit.*
Hull, Jeff. *Spoor.*
Jaramillo, Laura. *Material Girl.*

Lauture, Denize. *The Black Warrior and Other Poems.*
Lenhart, Gary. *Another Look: Selected Prose.*
Lyons, Kimberly. *The Practice of Residue.*
Malmude, Steve. *The Bundle: Selected Poems.*
McNally, John. *Exes for Eyes.*
Moxley, Jennifer. *The Middle Room: A Memoir.*
Nguyen, Hoa. *Your Ancient See Through.*
Olsen, Redell. *Punk Faun: A Bar Rock Pastel.*
Richards, Deborah. *Last One Out.*
Rothschild, Douglas. *Theogony.*
Sharma, Prageeta. *Bliss to Fill.*
Sinavaina-Gabbard, Caroline. *Alchemies of Distance.*
Stevens, James Thomas, & Caroline Sinavaiana. *Mohawk / Samoa: Transmigrations.*
Torres, Edwin. *Fractured Humorous.*
Wilkinson, John. *Oort's Cloud.*
Winter, Max. *Walking Among Them.*

Subpress Books are available through Small Press Distribution: www.spdbooks.org.